My Maine Thing

"Kennebunk is another name for Maine." My son Bruce said this when he was six. He was referring to the part of Maine we visit each summer. These pictures were all made within an easy ride by boat or car from Kennebunk Beach. This is where I grew up summers, where I learned to fish and swim and watched my children do the same.

A book can convey a sense of completeness and permanence, but in any book the reality goes just so far. In this book it is arbitrary and personal. There are no pictures here of super-straightened roads, overcrowded villages, horn-blowing motorists or bad-mannered boat-men. Here is the Kennebunk I think of when I'm far away.

I don't believe there are perfect people, places, or things, but I do believe there are perfect feelings. At Kennebunk, through all the stages of my life, I have found the ingredients of happiness. This book shows some of the people, places and things which have meant so much to me.

My MAINE Thing

B. A. King

B. A. King

for Sarah for christmas
from Beth.   1996

BLACK ICE PUBLISHERS

Design and production by Guy Russell
Duotones and separations by Carl Sesto
Typeset by Monotype Composition Co.

Library of Congress catalog no. 81-65328
ISBN 0-939250-00-4 Cloth
ISBN 0-939250-02-0 Special Edition

This book is dedicated to my grandmother, Alice Washburn. I thought she was a pain in the neck most of the time. She was forever reminding me to wear my rubbers, wash my hands, stand up straight and be nice to my sister. Sometimes she'd catch me going fishing before breakfast and make me go back to bed. But of all the people in her generation I think of her the most. She communicated excitement about special people from all backgrounds and was a romantic about the possibilities of life.

This picture is important to me. The child is Jennifer, our oldest, and she is doing what we all long to do. She has found a clean surface and is making her mark on it. To a child the sand is like a blank page to a writer or a hushed audience to a musician. That the page will burn, the people go home or the next wave wash away Jennifer's work is unimportant.

Kennebunk is an unsensational place. No unusual physical or cultural characteristics help me explain why I like the place and come back year after year. The feelings you have for a place are as much a reflection of you as they are of the place. Had I grown up in the mountains or beside a lake, had I caught my first fish and kissed my first girl there, I might have the same feelings for that place that I have now for Kennebunk.

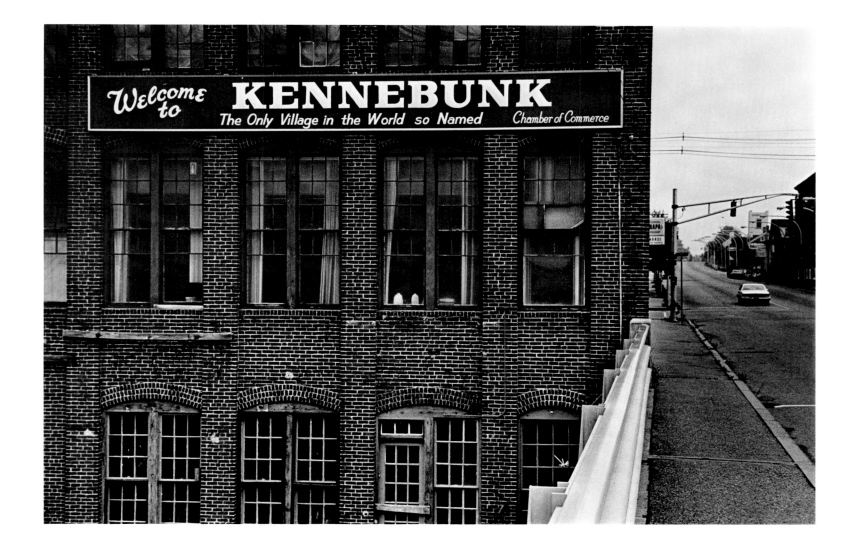

Perkins Cove at Ogunquit is a beautiful natural harbor, gem–like but dominated in summer by tourists and their boats (some people refer to it as the "bait bucket"). About twenty miles up the coast it is the other way around. Visitors to the wharf at Cape Porpoise approach the place and the fishermen on their best behavior.

Everyone used to know everyone else here—the summer and winter people, the young, the old and inbetween. Coming to Kennebunk summer after summer was like belonging to an extended family. Now there are so many visitors in the summer you couldn't begin to know them all, and the local folk have almost become curiosities.

In rental houses it's fun to examine the mixtures of furniture and tableware. You can't tell what was provided, forgotten or left behind on purpose. You wonder about the people who came before you and what their lives were like.

I never bring reading material with me when I visit a house that's been rented often because I like to sample the "grab bag" of literary debris which is almost always present—good stuff mixed with junk and odd specifics like a book about the steel industry or bobsledding. There's always the chance of something wonderful, a first edition or some volume beautifully illustrated.

* * * *

If you return to the same place again and again, you award yourself the status of old-timer. The place may be overcrowded and cut up, but because you know it well, you can still find wild and private places. When something new comes along, like a storm-blown bird, you appreciate the novelty of it.

There were always sea roses on the dining room table at Kennebunk. I know the women hurt their hands gathering those flowers. I never told anyone before how much I enjoyed them.

August people are August people and July people are July people. Many families come to the shore the same month every summer. Perhaps it's just inside my head, but there seems to be a difference between July and August people. They have been cleaning up after each other, yet ignoring each other, for years. They pass in the night on the highway during the last days of July, each smuggly confident that his month is superior to the other's.

It's hard to find places to rent these days around Kennebunk because more and more people have bought homes. What a lot of people do is to rent their house out for one month to cover costs and stay there the rest of the time themselves. I'm afraid the old hotels with their wide verandas and rows of rocking chairs looking out to sea are mostly torn down or out of business.

Dramas take place most often around the edges of things. A beach is an edge, a place where land and sea and sky come together, come apart. We enjoy thinking of beautiful summer beaches, but beaches are also habitats of violence. A beach, like a mountain, a desert or a jungle, is one of nature's extravagant gestures. A battleground in the wars of evolution, a place of change by conflict.

* * * *

People go to beaches to look and to be looked at. Weaknesses and strengths show up. Perhaps the kind of reality that exists on beaches quickens life there.

Some people revise their dietary habits in February, challenged by the thought of how they will look in their swimsuits come the Fourth of July.

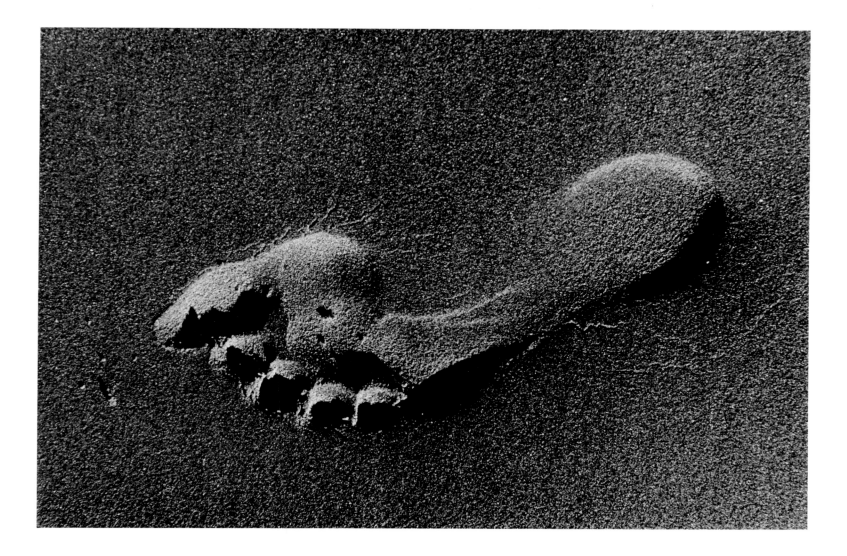

Some people prefer tides high. I like them low so I can see the sinews of the seashore and the small worlds in the pools at the bottom of things.

Life counts more if shared. When I am alone and find something special, some once-upon-a-time thing, like a child's gesture or the sound of pebbles rolling back from where a little wave has taken them, I wish someone were with me.

It's a nice feeling to be the first one on the beach.

The most innocent creatures I know are ocean sunfish. They weigh four to twelve hundred pounds, feed exclusively on plankton and are evolutionary throwbacks to eras before the appearance of man. Sunfish normally look half-dead as they proceed slowly, lolling from side to side. Their skin is like coarse sandpaper and, if you draw close, you can see what color boats have run into them and also how many times they have been gaffed "for sport." During the second World War the U.S. Navy issued orders to refrain from using them during depth charge practice.

You fish with someone and you get close. The fact that these fellows are fishless doesn't seem to bother them at all.

Kennebunk has been home to me more than anyplace else. Gulls have a certain cry they occasionally make which, whenever I hear it, no matter where I am, takes my thoughts rushing back there.

Cormorants are old fashioned birds, flying dinosaurs really, lacking an up-to-date feather lubricating system. When you see them perched with their wings outstretched in the sun, it is not arrogance: they have the laundry out to dry. They seem to fly underwater and are the kind of birds Asians have used for centuries for fishing. They tie them to strings and send them diving with a ring around their necks to prevent them from swallowing what they catch. Many people ignore cormorants and refer to them as sea crows or shags. Duck hunters train their dogs on them.

Cormorants are black with velvet brown epaulets (chevron–edged), green eyes, orange throats and purple tongues. They are unspeakably awkward and exquisitely graceful.

I love terns. Everything about them amazes me. They appear to be made of air, light and gristle and are the essence of *birdness*. They migrate to the far reaches of South America and nest on the very edge of the earth on sand spits and low reefs. After a full moon's high tides I have found the eggs from entire tern colonies washed together with seaweed and muscle shells, cracked and stinking.

There is little in favor of terns today except their immaculate wildness, which at times is also their undoing. Possessing extraordinary individual and collective bravery, they attack whatever approaches their nesting area and will dive to within inches of your face, sometimes even knocking your hat off. Unfortunately, people sometimes take their bravery as a challenge and respond to the acrobatics and marvelous flying show by throwing stones.

There were many terns around Kennebunk when I was young. Now there are many more gulls, who thrive on man's protection, handouts and garbage.

Lighthouses are found in some of the world's most beautiful, dangerous and least accessible places. Their purpose is as simple as it is noble—to cast light and sound to keep people from harm. People who live in such beautiful and demanding places are often interesting; beauty and drama encircling you constantly either make you more alive or kill you slowly.

Lighthouse keepers live in relentless and insistent close proximity to one another. I knew of two who hated each other and never spoke. When one forgot to turn on the light and foghorn, the other wouldn't tell him or do it for him.

Lighthouses are being automated and that means fewer and fewer keepers. When the Coast Guard decided to automate the Goat Island Light at Cape Porpoise a few years ago, the lobster fishermen made a fuss. Lighthouse keepers do plenty of things besides turning on the equipment, such as help small boats in trouble or radio for assistance in emergencies. They can be like guardian angels.

The sea has a glamour with which it touches all those who live by it. The lobsterman in the East is something like the cowboy in the West: little boys grow up wanting to be one. With their vivid language, rusted pickup trucks and small boats (marvels of grace and maneuverability), the lobstermen bring class and excitement to the little harbors of Southern Maine.

A successful lobsterman is a combination of skill and endurance, wisdom and cunning. Each day he knows whether he has done well and so does everyone else at the dock.

Lobstermen are superstitious, and two of the things they are superstitious about are the color blue and pigs. They won't tie up beside a blue boat or let anyone aboard who is wearing blue. If pigs are mentioned or a ham sandwich is eaten on board they will turn around and go in. I knew an old man who ate his lunch every day at the same cove. One morning he had a fight with his wife and when he opened his lunch that day he found she had drawn a pig on his hard-boiled egg. He threw his lunch and lunchbox overboard and never went back to that cove.

The atmosphere of a Maine wharf is dominated by lobster bait—the smell of it, the space it takes up, and the work it takes to move bait barrels on and off boats. At most wharfs there is a ragged band of cats which feeds at night on the rotting fish and disappears in the morning with the arrival of the first lobstermen.

In Maine there is someone around to profit by whatever happens. It is a fact of nature that men's dreams are in conflict with one another. Sea moss gatherers pray for storms to tear loose quantities of sea moss which can be gathered easily at the next low tide and sold as a thickener to the food, cosmetic and fertilizer companies. Whenever the mossmen's prayers come true, lobstermen lose equipment and many lobsters.

Clifford Jackson's place is called Snug Harbor Farm. There are hollyhocks growing outside the front door and you can hear the sea from any corner of it, especially when the wind is from the east. Mr. Jackson raises a variety of animals for personal needs and vegetables and strawberries for selling at his roadside stand (Sound Horn).

You can take in the whole farm with one good look—the deep woodlot, the long grass swamp where the cattle go on hot afternoons, a small pond for ducks and geese and fire protection, a little hill, a meadow, one beehive and perhaps the world's smallest apple orchard (seven trees). There is an agreeable assortment of outbuildings, and the barn itself is connected in perfect proportion to the little white house where Bell and Clifford Jackson live.

The place is a living museum. Antique equipment, well-loved and in working order, is stored conveniently in and around the buildings. All the work on the place is done by hand or horse or oxen.

There are sometimes deer in the cornfield at daybreak or killdeer nesting among the strawberries (never more than four eggs). But the most interesting thing on the place is Farmer Jackson himself. He never stops moving and he never hurries. When I watch him work I begin to understand how clearings were made in our unforgiving New England terrain, emptied of stones and boulders and turned into fields with stone walls around them.

My memories of rainy days in Maine are happy: wood smoke, wool sweaters, marshmallows, once in a while a movie at the Lyric Theater with the sound of the tides lapping at the pilings underneath.

In summer you are looking for what is missing in your winters—love, adventure, some lucky strike. It is a time for miracles—learning to swim, discovering a thrush's nest. I've seen pudgy little girls come home at summer's end slender and all grown up.

Summer is a time for afternoon naps and shooting stars, a time for crowds and solitude, a time for doing and not doing much. It is a time for considering your options and dreaming dreams, a time for exploring new territory and for enjoying the familiar.

The babysitter is an important figure in the life of a family with young children. We have had good ones and bad ones. The good ones, like Molly and Sara, became like daughters and we still see them from time to time. It pleases me to see our own two daughters wanting to be mother's helpers. It is a wonderful way to learn about how other people live and to gain more authority and responsibility than they are accustomed to at home.

Winter affects everything in Maine. On the prettiest summer day its influence is all around you in the shape of things. In Maine there are the rocks, the wind, the water and the winter. *What are you going to do when it comes off snappy?*

"If you live in Maine you don't have to travel. You're already there," Faye, a salesgirl at L.L. Bean, said to some customers who bet she'd never been to New York.